bite-sized

Spain

First published in 2000 by Hamlyn an imprint of
Octopus Publishing Group Limited
2–4 Heron Quays, London E14 4JP

British Library Cataloguing-in-Publication Data
A catalogue record for this book is available from the
British Library

ISBN 0 600 60060 2

Produced by Toppan
Printed in China

Editors: Sharyn Conlan and Anne Crane
Proofreader: Joanna Smith
Creative Director: Keith Martin
Designer: David Godfrey
Production Controller: Lisa Moore
Picture Researcher: Rosie Garai
Indexer: Hilary Bird

Photography acknowledgements
Octopus Publishing Group Ltd./W. Adams-Lingwood 68-69/Jean Cazals 32-33
/Sandra Lane title, 4 left, 4 right, 5 right, 6 left, 6 Centre, 7 right, 7 Centre, 8 left,
14, 15, 17, 23, 24, 27, 29, 35, 42, 43, 53, 72, 76, 77, 79 /James Merrell 5 left, 46,
50-51 /Neil Mersh 9 left, 25, 44 /Sean Myers 7 left, 12-13, 36, 58-59 /Ian Wallace
5 Bottom Left, 6 right, 8 right, 8 Centre, 9 right, 9 Centre, 16, 31, 39, 48, 57, 64-65,
67 /Philip Webb 21, 26
Axiom Photographic Agency/Alberto Arzoz 40-41, Guggenheim Museum,
Bilbao/ Steve Benbow 10-11, Back Cover, La Sagrada Família, Barcelona
Corbis UK Ltd/Catherine Karnow 18-19, detail of a bullfighter/ Hulton-Deutsch
Collection 74-75, flamenco dancer
Spanish National Tourist Office 54-55, Spanish flag

Notes
Standard level spoon measurements are used in all recipes.
1 tablespoon = one 15 ml spoon
1 teaspoon = one 5 ml spoon

Both metric and imperial measurements have been given in all recipes.
Use one set of measurements only and not a mixture of both.

Eggs should be medium unless otherwise stated.

Fresh herbs should be used unless otherwise stated. If unavailable use
dried herbs as an alternative but halve the quantities stated.

Do not re-freeze a dish that has been frozen previously.

Ovens should be preheated to the specified temperature – if using a
fan-assisted oven, follow the manufacturer's instructions for adjusting the
time and temperature.

bite-sized
Spain

contents

3

These dishes come somewhere between a starter and a light meal. They include such delights as Stuffed Baby Squid and Marinated Sardines.

5

This chapter contains a selection of sauces and salsas to serve as an accompaniment or for dipping.

4

Here you will find some more substantial classic Spanish dishes, such as Paella and Kidneys Cooked with Sherry.

introduction

The concept of bite-sized eating comes naturally to the Spanish. After all, they could be said to have invented it back in the nineteenth century, when the custom of eating tapas, or small snacks, with a glass of chilled sherry or wine began. Literally translated, the word *tapa* means a cover and originally referred to the slice of bread which bar owners would place over a glass of wine to prevent insects getting into the drink. In time, they started to put slices of ham or cheese on top of the bread and so the custom began, or so the story goes. Nowadays refinement and sophistication have entered the picture. The modern Spanish custom is to go out before lunch or dinner to meet friends and saunter from bar to bar, enjoying stimulating conversation while nibbling a wide range of snacks and sipping wine. True tapas are finger food, although cocktail sticks and forks may be used for spearing, but they are never knife and fork food.

Tapas are also a very practical option when entertaining at home; they are perfect for drinks parties, or can take the place of a more formal first course at a dinner party. *Bite-sized Spain* goes further still; in this book the appetizers and snacks grow larger and more substantial chapter by chapter, culminating in Little Meals, a selection of dishes for light lunches and informal suppers when just one dish – or perhaps a choice of several different dishes all served at the same time – seems to suit the occasion. Nibbles, the first chapter, is just that, a series of tantalizing tasters such as marinated olives – the great Spanish passion – and salted almonds, perfect with a glass of chilled wine, and all gone in a single delicious mouthful. Bigger Bites are just that much larger. They include the classic Spanish tortilla and a more elaborate tortilla with red pepper, both of which can be served in pieces of varying size according to what best suits the occasion. There are also fried calamares, accompanied by a

dipping sauce; and Manchego fritters, deep-fried cheese balls made with Spain's best-known cheese. This chapter also includes some sweet recipes, such as Churros, deep-fried orange-flavoured batter fingers, which the Spanish enjoy for breakfast with hot chocolate or coffee; and Tarta de Naranja, a delectable orange and almond custard tart. The dishes in A Bite More are almost little meals: Empanadas Gallegas are the Spanish answer to the Cornish pasty substantial turnovers filled with a delicious mixture of fish and ham; and Albondigas, meatballs which can be speared as a cocktail savoury or served as a meal with a spicy tomato sauce. Finally, there are Salsas and Dips, perfect to accompany many of the recipes.

Spanish cooking has deep Arab roots. The Moorish invasion of Spain began in July 711 when the Moors, a mixed Arab and Berber people from North Africa, landed in Andalusia. They occupied Spain for over 700 years and their influence on all aspects of Spanish life has been enormous, not least of all in the kitchen. The introduction of almonds, aubergines, spinach, oranges and lemons, mint, and spices such as cinnamon, allspice, saffron, cumin and coriander are all due to them, so too is the cultivation of sugar and rice in the south of Spain, and those vital kitchen implements, the pestle and mortar. The Moors were driven out by Ferdinand II of Aragon, the king who with his wife Isabella of Castile backed the Genoese explorer Christopher Columbus on his voyages to the West Indies and the Americas. From these voyages he returned with tomatoes, potatoes and peppers, without which Spanish cooking, and the cooking of the rest of Europe, would be truly deficient.

Spanish cooking is robust, rich and colourful – red and green peppers, oranges and saffron-yellow paella spring to mind. Listed overleaf are some of the foods which are particularly associated with Spain.

glossary

Allioli
Sometimes spelled alioli, this is the Spanish version (some say the origin) of the Provençal aïoli, an oil, garlic and egg yolk sauce. Like mayonnaise, allioli is served with cold dishes or as a dipping sauce.

Bacalao
A legacy of the Middle Ages, this is dried salt cod, which must be soaked for 24 hours in several changes of cold water before it is cooked. A Spanish passion, bacalao is ranked in the same class as smoked salmon.

Cheese
Manchego, from La Mancha, is Spain's best-known cheese. Made with ewe's milk, it has a firm texture with tiny holes and is sold in matured and medium matured versions. It may be pasteurised or unpasteurised. Idiazabal, another ewe's milk cheese, is a robust, sharp-flavoured cheese from the Basque region. Valdeón and Picos de Europa are soft, creamy blue cheeses; Valdeón is made from cow's milk, or a mix of cow's and goat's milk, while Picos, is made with cow's milk.

Chorizo
A spicy pork sausage flavoured with garlic and paprika, making it a distinctive red colour. Chorizo may be mild or highly spiced; it is usually cured and eaten raw.

Escabèche
An Arab word for a cooking technique in which fish and vegetables are cooked in wine or vinegar and then marinated in the cooking liquid or in another marinade.

Olives and Olive oil

The olive tree has been cultivated around the Mediterranean since the beginning of recorded history. Spain grows more than 50 types of olive and is one of the world's largest producers of olive oil. In general, Spanish oils are fragrant and fruity.

Saffron

This spice comes from the purple *Crocus sativus*, which has long yellow stamens. The best is reputed to come from La Mancha; the flowers appear overnight sometime around the middle of October and must be picked by hand the same day. The rich yellow pistils and stamens are removed and toasted over charcoal to produce saffron. The picking is a back-breaking task – a long day's work yields only about 50–75 g (2–3 oz) of saffron. The world's most precious spice, by weight saffron is more expensive than gold.

Serrano ham

Cured, air-dried raw ham from acorn-fed pigs reared in the oak forests of south-west Spain. The very best Serrano ham comes from special black-legged pigs.

Tortilla

The Spanish tortilla is a deep omelette, often containing vegetables, which has more in common with Italian frittata than thin, light French omelettes. It has no connection with the Mexican tortilla.

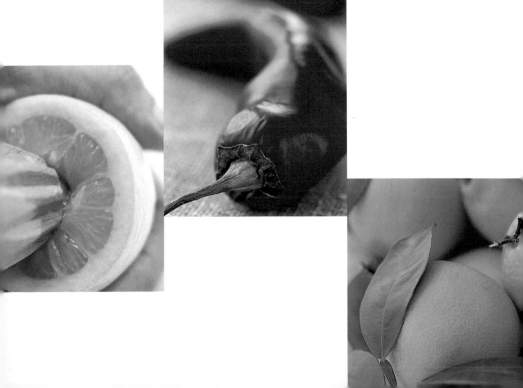

1

nibbles

deep-fried onion rings
in beer batter

salted almonds

spicy glazed cashews

chorizo with bread

marinated olives

Serves 4–6 / **Preparation time** 10 minutes / **Cooking time** 10 minutes

deep-fried onion rings in beer batter
aros de cebolla al batido de cerveza

- **4 large white or red Spanish onions**
- **vegetable oil, for deep-frying**
- **a few snipped chives or tarragon, to garnish**
- **Allioli, to serve (see page 77)**

BATTER
- **1 egg, separated**
- **1 tablespoon olive oil**
- **100 ml (3½ fl oz) light ale or lager**
- **65 g (2½ oz) plain flour**
- **salt and pepper**

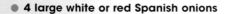

1. Cut the onions into 5 mm (¼ inch) thick slices and separate the rings. Reserve all the larger rings and discard the rest or keep them for use in another recipe.

2. Beat together the egg yolk, oil, beer and flour in a bowl and season to taste with salt and pepper. In another bowl, whisk the egg white until stiff then fold it into the batter until evenly incorporated.

3. Heat 5 cm (2 inches) of vegetable oil in a deep saucepan until it reaches 180–190°C (350–375°F), or until a cube of bread browns in 30 seconds. Dip the onion rings, a few at a time, into the batter and then into the oil and deep-fry for 1–2 minutes until golden. Remove with a slotted spoon and drain on kitchen paper.

4. Serve the onion rings hot, garnished with chives or tarragon, and with allioli to dip.

salted
almonds
almendras saladas

- **6 tablespoons olive oil**
- **250 g (8 oz) blanched almonds**
- **sea salt**

1 Heat the oil in a small, heavy-based frying pan, add the nuts in several batches and stir-fry over a moderate heat until evenly browned.

2 Transfer the nuts to a serving bowl with a slotted spoon. Add plenty of sea salt and stir to coat the nuts. Although these nuts are better eaten straight away, they can be stored in an airtight container for up to 3 days.

Serves 4 / **Preparation time** 5 minutes / **Cooking time** about 10 minutes

Serves 4 / **Preparation time** 5 minutes + cooling / **Cooking time** 5–10 minutes

spicy glazed cashews
marañones picantes glaseados

- **25 g (1 oz) unsalted butter**
- **3 tablespoons clear honey**
- **1 teaspoon salt**
- **¼ teaspoon cayenne pepper**
- **1 tablespoon water**
- **250 g (8 oz) cashew nuts**

1 Melt the butter in a small, heavy-based frying pan and then stir in the honey, salt, cayenne pepper and water. Bring to the boil.

2 Add the cashew nuts and stir over a moderate heat for 5 minutes until the nuts are toasted and well coated with the glaze.

3 Tip out on to a greased baking sheet and leave to cool. These nuts are best eaten the day they are cooked.

Serves 4 / **Preparation time** 15 minutes / **Cooking time** 5 minutes

chorizo
with bread
chorizo con pan

- **250 g (8 oz) piece of mild chorizo sausage**
- **3 tablespoons extra virgin olive oil**
- **1 garlic clove, sliced**
- **¼ teaspoon dried chilli flakes**
- **2 slices of country bread, cubed**

1 Cut the chorizo into 5 mm (¼ inch) thick slices. Heat the oil in a small frying pan, add the garlic and dried chilli flakes and fry gently for about 1 minute until they release their aroma. Do not let them burn.

2 Strain the oil and return to the pan. Add the chorizo and stir-fry for 1–2 minutes until golden. Remove with a slotted spoon.

3 Toss the bread cubes briefly in the pan juices and drain. Spear each slice of sausage on a cocktail stick with a cube of bread and serve immediately.

marinated olives

aceitunas en escabèche

- **500 g (1 lb) green or black olives**
- **1 red chilli, deseeded and chopped**
- **4 garlic cloves, crushed**
- **1 oregano sprig**
- **1 thyme sprig**
- **1 teaspoon finely chopped rosemary**
- **2 bay leaves**
- **1 teaspoon fennel seeds, bruised**
- **1 teaspoon roasted and finely crushed cumin seeds**
- **olive oil, to cover**

1 Using a small sharp knife, make a lengthways slit through to the stone of each olive. Put the olives into a bowl and stir in the chilli, garlic, oregano, thyme, rosemary, bay leaves, fennel seeds and cumin.

2 Pack the olive mixture into a screw-top jar and cover completely with olive oil. Close the jar tightly and leave the olives for at least 3 days, shaking the jar occasionally, before using. If stored in a cool, dark place the olives will keep for several months.

Serves 4 / **Preparation time** 20 minutes + marinating

2

bigger bites

Serves 8 / **Preparation time** 10 minutes + resting/ **Cooking time** 30 minutes

classic spanish omelette

tortilla español

- **150 ml (¼ pint) extra virgin olive oil**
- **750 g (1½ lb) potatoes, thinly sliced**
- **1 large onion, sliced**
- **5 large eggs, beaten**
- **salt and pepper**

1 Heat all but 2 tablespoons of the oil in a 20 cm (8 inch) nonstick frying pan. Add the potato and onion slices and cook, stirring frequently, for 15 minutes until the vegetables are golden and just tender.

2 Stir the potato mixture into the beaten eggs and season generously with salt and pepper. Set aside for 15 minutes. Clean the frying pan.

3 Heat the remaining oil in the clean pan and tip in the tortilla mixture. Cook over a low heat for 10 minutes until almost cooked through. Carefully slide the tortilla on to a large plate. Invert another plate over the tortilla and turn the plates upside down so that you can slide the tortilla back into the frying pan, cooked side uppermost.

4 Return the pan to the heat and cook for 5 minutes or until the tortilla is cooked on both sides. Leave to cool then serve the tortilla at room temperature, cut into wedges or squares.

This is a traditional Spanish tortilla which is made with eggs, potatoes and onions. It is cooked in a large quantity of olive oil.

omelette with red pepper

*tortilla de
pimiento rojo*

- **150 ml (¼ pint) extra virgin olive oil**
- **750 g (1½ lb) potatoes, thinly sliced**
- **1 Spanish onion, chopped**
- **1 large red pepper, cored, deseeded and sliced**
- **1 green pepper, cored, deseeded and sliced**
- **5 large eggs, beaten**
- **salt and pepper**

1 Heat all but 2 tablespoons of the oil in a 20 cm (8 inch) nonstick frying pan. Add the potato slices, onion and red and green peppers and cook, stirring frequently, for 15 minutes, until all the vegetables are golden and tender.

2 Stir the potato mixture into a large bowl containing the beaten eggs and season generously with salt and pepper. Set aside for 15 minutes. Clean the frying pan.

3 Heat the remaining oil in the clean pan and tip in the tortilla mixture. Cook over a low heat for 10 minutes, until almost cooked through. Carefully slide the tortilla on to a large plate. Invert another plate over the tortilla and turn the plates upside down so that you can slide the tortilla back into the frying pan, cooked side uppermost.

4 Return the pan to the heat and cook for a further 5 minutes, or until the tortilla is cooked on both sides. Leave to cool then serve the tortilla at room temperature, cut into wedges or squares.

Serves 8 / **Preparation time** 10 minutes + resting / **Cooking time** 30 minutes

Serves 8 / **Preparation time** 15 minutes / **Cooking time** 30–40 minutes

chickpea and chard omelette
tortilla de garbanzos y verdura

- **6 tablespoons extra virgin olive oil**
- **1 onion, chopped**
- **4 garlic cloves, crushed**
- **½ teaspoon crushed chilli flakes**
- **500 g (1 lb) chard leaves**
- **400 g (13 oz) can chickpeas, drained**
- **6 eggs, beaten**
- **2 tablespoons chopped parsley**
- **salt and pepper**

1 Heat 4 tablespoons of oil in a large, heavy-based nonstick frying pan. Add the onion, garlic and chilli flakes and fry gently for 10 minutes until softened and lightly golden.

2 Meanwhile, wash and dry the chard and cut away and discard the thick white central stalk. Shred the leaves. Stir the chard and chickpeas into the onion mixture and cook gently for 5 minutes.

3 Beat the eggs in a bowl, add the parsley and season with salt and pepper. Stir in the chickpea mixture.

4 Wipe out the pan, then add the remaining oil. Pour in the egg and chickpea mixture and cook over a low heat for 10 minutes until the tortilla is almost cooked through.

5 Carefully slide the tortilla on to a large plate, invert the pan over the tortilla and then flip it back into the pan.

6 Return the pan to the heat for 5 minutes until the tortilla is cooked through. Leave it to cool to room temperature and serve cut into wedges or squares.

broad beans with serrano ham
habas con jamon serrano

- **1 tablespoon olive oil**
- **125 g (4 oz) piece of Serrano ham, diced**
- **2 garlic cloves, sliced**
- **250 g (8 oz) freshly podded broad beans or 750 g (1½ lb) in the pod**
- **75 ml (3½ fl oz) dry white wine**
- **2 tomatoes, skinned, deseeded and diced**
- **1 tablespoon chopped dill**
- **salt and pepper**

1 Heat the oil in a small, heavy-based frying pan, add the ham and fry briefly to brown it all over. Lower the heat, add the garlic and broad beans and fry gently for 5 minutes.

2 Add the wine and diced tomatoes and bring to the boil. Cover the pan and simmer for 10–15 minutes until the beans are tender.

3 Season to taste with salt and pepper, stir in the dill and serve immediately.

Serves 4 / **Preparation time** 12 minutes / **Cooking time** 15–20 minutes

chorizo with beans and herbs

chorizo con habas y hierbas

- **250 g (8 oz) freshly podded broad beans or 750 g (1½ lb) in the pod**
- **125 g (4 oz) spicy chorizo sausage**
- **1 tablespoon olive oil**
- **2 garlic cloves, roughly chopped**
- **1 tablespoon chopped dill**
- **1 tablespoon chopped mint**
- **2 tablespoons lemon juice**
- **salt and pepper**
- **crusty bread, to serve**

1 Blanch the beans in lightly salted boiling water for 1 minute then drain and refresh under cold water. Dry well.

2 Cut the sausage into slices about 5 mm (¼ inch) thick. Heat the oil in a frying pan, add the garlic pieces and fry gently for 2–3 minutes until softened, then discard. Increase the heat, add the sliced chorizo and stir-fry for about 2–3 minutes until it is golden and has released some of its oil.

3 Stir in the beans and cook for a further 2–3 minutes, then add the herbs, squeeze over the lemon juice and season to taste with salt and pepper. Serve warm with crusty bread.

Tapas bars serve this dish, or similar versions of it, all over Spain. It is quick and easy to prepare, and delicious with a glass of chilled wine.

Serves 4–6 / **Preparation time** 8 minutes / **Cooking time** about 10 minutes

paprika potatoes
patatas bravas

- **1 kg (2 lb) small potatoes**
- **2 tablespoons olive oil**
- **sea salt**

SAUCE
- **4 tablespoons olive oil**
- **1 tablespoon tomato purée**
- **1 tablespoon red wine vinegar**
- **2 tablespoons water**
- **1 teaspoon chilli sauce**
- **2 teaspoons paprika**
- **salt and pepper**

1 Cut the potatoes into 1 cm (½ inch) thick slices and place in a single layer on a baking sheet.

2 Brush with olive oil, sprinkle with sea salt and roast in a preheated oven, 230°C (450°F), Gas Mark 8, for 20 minutes. Turn the potatoes over and bake for a further 10 minutes or until crisp and golden brown.

3 Meanwhile, combine all the sauce ingredients in a sauté pan and stir together. Add the cooked potatoes and heat through. Season to taste with salt and pepper and serve hot.

Serves 8 / **Preparation time** 10 minutes / **Cooking time** about 30 minutes

grilled mushrooms with garlic oil

champiñones a la plancha
con aceite al ajillo

- **75 ml (3 fl oz) extra virgin olive oil**
- **2 garlic cloves, crushed**
- **grated rind and juice of ½ lime**
- **1 small red chilli, deseeded and finely chopped**
- **2 tablespoons chopped parsley**
- **12 large flat mushrooms**
- **salt and pepper**

1 Combine all the ingredients except the mushrooms in a small bowl and season to taste with salt and pepper.

2 Arrange the mushrooms stalk side down on a foil-lined grill pan and cook under a preheated grill, as close to the heat as possible, for 3–4 minutes until their juices are beginning to run.

3 Flip the mushrooms over and cook for a further 4–5 minutes until cooked through. Transfer to a warmed serving platter and pour over the dressing. Leave to cool to room temperature before serving.

(In this recipe the large, succulent mushrooms are grilled before being dressed with the garlic oil, which intensifies their flavour.)

Serves 6 / **Preparation time** 5 minutes + cooling / **Cooking time** 8–10 minutes

fried manchego cheese fritters
manchego frito

- olive oil, for deep-frying
- 2 egg whites
- 125 g (4 oz) mature Manchego cheese, finely grated
- 50 g (2 oz) fresh breadcrumbs
- about 1 tablespoon finely chopped herbs, such as parsley, chives and thyme
- paprika
- salt and pepper

1 Heat the olive oil in a deep-fryer or large saucepan to 180–190°C (350–375°F), or until a cube of bread browns in 30 seconds.

2 Meanwhile, in a bowl, whisk the egg whites until stiff but not dry. Using a large metal spoon, lightly fold in the grated cheese, breadcrumbs and herbs. Season with salt, pepper and paprika. Form the cheese mixture into small walnut-sized balls.

3 Add the cheese balls to the hot oil in batches, taking care not to overcrowd the pan, and fry for about 3 minutes until golden. When the fritters are ready, transfer them to kitchen paper with a slotted spoon to drain. Serve hot.

Serves 4–6 / **Preparation time** 10 minutes / **Cooking time** about 15 minutes

deep-fried artichokes *alcachofas fritas*

- **12 baby artichokes**
- **1 lemon, halved**
- **vegetable oil, for deep-frying**
- **4 tablespoons seasoned flour**
- **lemon wedges, to garnish**
- **salt, to serve**

1 Trim the artichokes and cut lengthways in half or quarters depending on their size. Rub all over the cut surfaces with the halved lemon.

2 Heat 5 cm (2 inches) of vegetable oil in a deep-fryer or large saucepan to 180–190°C (350–375°F), or until a cube of bread browns in 30 seconds.

3 Dip the artichokes in the seasoned flour until well coated and deep-fry in batches for 1–2 minutes until crisp and golden. Drain on kitchen paper. Serve sprinkled with salt and garnished with lemon wedges.

Serves 8 / **Preparation time** 15 minutes + cooling /
Cooking time about 55 minutes

prawn, rice and bean croquettes

croquetas de gambas, arroz y judias

- 15 g (½ oz) butter
- 1 garlic clove, crushed
- 2 shallots, finely chopped
- 125 g (4 oz) Spanish short-grain or risotto rice
- 600 ml (1 pint) hot fish or vegetable stock
- 125 g (4 oz) cooked peeled prawns, roughly chopped
- 125 g (4 oz) green beans, finely chopped
- 2 tablespoons chopped mint
- 2 tablespoons freshly grated Parmesan cheese
- 2 eggs, lightly beaten
- 4 tablespoons seasoned flour
- 50 g (2 oz) fresh white breadcrumbs
- vegetable oil, for deep-frying
- salt and pepper
- chopped chives or coriander, to garnish
- soured cream, to serve

1 Melt the butter in a saucepan and fry the garlic and shallots for 5 minutes. Add the rice and stir-fry for 30 seconds.

2 Add a ladleful of stock and simmer until absorbed. Continue adding stock, a ladleful at a time, and stirring the rice, for about 20 minutes until almost all the stock is absorbed.

3 With the final ladleful of stock add the prawns and beans, cover and cook for 5–10 minutes until the rice is tender.

4 Remove the saucepan from the heat, stir in the chopped mint and grated Parmesan and season to taste with salt and pepper. Cover the surface with greaseproof paper and set aside to cool.

5 Beat in half the beaten eggs, half the seasoned flour and 3 tablespoons of the breadcrumbs. Form the mixture into 5 cm (2 inch) balls. Dust the croquettes with the remaining seasoned flour, dip into the remaining egg and then coat with the remaining breadcrumbs.

6 Heat 5 cm (2 inches) of oil in a deep saucepan until it reaches 180–190°C (350–375°F), or until a cube of bread browns in 30 seconds.

7 Deep-fry the croquettes in batches for 1–2 minutes until golden. Drain on kitchen paper and keep warm in a hot oven while frying the rest. Garnish with the chives or coriander and serve warm with soured cream.

Serves 4 / **Preparation time** 15 minutes / **Cooking time** 5–10 minutes

prawns with garlic and chillies

gambas con ajo y picante

- **100 ml (3½ fl oz) olive oil**
- **4-5 garlic cloves, finely crushed**
- **1 red chilli, deseeded and chopped**
- **500 g (1 lb) raw prawns, peeled**
- **2-3 tablespoons chopped parsley**
- **sea salt**

TO SERVE
- **lemon wedges**
- **4 slices of country bread**

1 Heat the oil in 4 individual flameproof earthenware dishes over a high heat. Add the garlic and chilli, cook for about 1-2 minutes, then add the prawns and sea salt to taste. Cook briskly for about 2-3 minutes, shaking the dishes frequently. Stir in the parsley and serve the sizzling prawns with lemon wedges and bread to mop up the juices.

Tip The generous amount of oil in which the prawns are cooked should still be actively sizzling when they are served, so that they stay crisp and dry.

salt cod fritters
bacalao frito

- **250 g (8 oz) salt cod**
- **150 ml (¼ pint) milk**
- **250 g (8 oz) potatoes, cubed**
- **1 garlic clove, crushed**
- **2 spring onions, finely chopped**
- **1 tablespoon chopped coriander leaves**
- **1 egg yolk**
- **oil, for shallow-frying**
- **pepper**
- **Allioli (see page 77) or mayonnaise, to serve**

TO GARNISH
- **shredded lemon rind**
- **coriander sprigs**

1 Put the salt cod into a large bowl and cover with cold water. Leave to soak for 24 hours, changing the water several times.

2 Drain the cod and dry well. Remove the skin and bones and cut the flesh into small cubes. Place in a bowl, cover with the milk and leave for 2 hours.

3 Drain the cod and place it in a saucepan with the potatoes. Cover with water, bring to the boil and simmer, covered, for 20 minutes until the cod and potatoes are tender.

4 Drain the fish and potatoes and mash together. Beat in all the remaining ingredients except for the oil, and season with pepper.

5 Heat about 2.5 cm (1 inch) of oil in a deep frying pan. Drop teaspoons of the cod mixture into the oil and fry the fritters in batches for 1–2 minutes until they are browned on all sides.

6 As the fritters are done, drain them on kitchen paper and keep them warm while frying the rest. Garnish with lemon rind and coriander and serve with allioli or mayonnaise.

Serves 8 / **Preparation time** 35 minutes + soaking / **Cooking time** 30 minutes

Serves 8 / **Preparation time** 15 minutes / **Cooking time** about 10 minutes

deep-fried calamares

calamares fritos

- **500 g (1 lb) small squid, cleaned**

- **vegetable oil, for deep-frying**

- **2 eggs, lightly beaten**

- **2–4 tablespoons flour, seasoned with salt, pepper and a pinch of cayenne pepper**

TO SERVE

- **sea salt**

- **lemon juice**

- **Allïoli (see page 77)**

1 Cut the squid into rings and halve the tentacles. Wash well and dry thoroughly on kitchen paper.

2 Heat 5 cm (2 inches) of vegetable oil in a deep saucepan until it reaches 180–190°C (350–375°F), or until a cube of bread browns in 30 seconds.

3 Meanwhile, dip the squid into the beaten egg and coat with the seasoned flour. Deep-fry in batches for 1–2 minutes until crisp and golden then drain on kitchen paper. Keep the cooked squid warm in a hot oven while cooking the remainder. Serve hot, sprinkled with sea salt, drizzled with lemon juice and accompanied by a bowl of allioli.

grilled
mussels
mejillones a la plancha

- **20 large fresh mussels, scrubbed**
- **25 g (1 oz) basil leaves**
- **1 garlic clove, crushed**
- **1 small red chilli, deseeded and diced**
- **½ teaspoon grated lemon rind**
- **1 tablespoon pine nuts**
- **1 tablespoon freshly grated Manchego or Parmesan cheese**
- **2 tablespoons fresh breadcrumbs**
- **3-4 tablespoons extra virgin olive oil**
- **salt and pepper**

1 Remove any beards still attached to the mussels. Tip the mussels into a saucepan and steam them with just the water on their shells for 4 minutes until they open. Discard any which do not open. Immediately plunge the mussels into cold water; then drain thoroughly.

2 Discard the empty half of each shell and arrange the mussels in a large dish or 4 individual gratin dishes.

3 Combine the basil, garlic, chilli, lemon rind, pine nuts, cheese and half of the breadcrumbs in a food processor or blender and pulse briefly to form a smooth paste. Season to taste with salt and pepper.

4 Transfer the basil paste to a bowl and stir in the oil. Spoon a little of the paste over each mussel and top each one with a few more breadcrumbs. Cook under a preheated grill for 2–3 minutes or until bubbling and golden. Serve immediately.

Serves 4–6 / **Preparation time** 10 minutes / **Cooking time** 20 minutes

fried doughnuts
churros

- **150 g (5 oz) butter**
- **300 ml (½ pint) water**
- **150 g (5 oz) flour**
- **3 eggs, plus 1 egg yolk**
- **grated rind of 1 orange**
- **oil, for deep-frying**
- **1 tablespoon ground cinnamon**
- **150 g (5 oz) caster sugar**

1 Cut the butter into pieces and put the pieces into a large saucepan with the water. Heat the water gently until the butter melts; then bring to a rolling boil.

2 Sift the flour at least twice and, as soon as the water boils, tip it into the pan. Remove from the heat and beat the flour into the butter and water. Continue beating until the mixture forms a ball and leaves the sides of the pan clean. Allow to cool a little and then beat in the eggs, the extra yolk and the orange rind.

3 Spoon the mixture into a nylon piping bag fitted with a large star nozzle. Pipe it into 15 cm (6 inch) lengths. In a large, heavy-based saucepan, heat the oil for deep-frying to 180–190°C (350–375°F) or until a cube of bread browns in 30 seconds.

4 Deep-fry the doughnuts a few at a time until they are golden brown, turning them once. Remove them from the oil with a slotted spoon and drain on kitchen paper.

5 Mix together the cinnamon and sugar and sprinkle over the warm doughnuts.

Serves 4 / **Preparation time** 25 minutes + standing / **Cooking time** 10–15 minutes

banana fritters
plátano frito

- **4 firm ripe bananas, peeled and cut in half**
- **4 tablespoons lemon juice**
- **4 tablespoons Spanish brandy**
- **flour, for dusting**
- **oil, for deep-frying**
- **3 tablespoons icing sugar**

BATTER
- **50 g (2 oz) plain flour**
- **pinch of salt**
- **1 egg, lightly beaten**
- **1 tablespoon melted butter**
- **6 tablespoons milk**
- **1 egg white**

1 Put the bananas into a shallow dish with the lemon juice and brandy. Stir, then set aside for 20 minutes.

2 Meanwhile, prepare the batter. Sift the flour and salt into a large mixing bowl. Beat in the beaten egg, butter and milk and mix until the batter is quite smooth. Whisk the egg white until fairly stiff and fold it lightly into the batter.

3 Drain the banana pieces on kitchen paper and dust them with flour, then dip each one into the batter. Heat the oil in a deep-fryer or large saucepan to 180–190°C (350–375°F), or until a cube of bread browns in 30 seconds. Lower the banana pieces into the pan and deep-fry in batches for 3–4 minutes or until crisp and golden.

4 Drain the banana fritters thoroughly on kitchen paper then dust immediately with a generous dredging of icing sugar. Serve piping hot.

Serves 10 / **Preparation time** 15 minutes / **Cooking time** 30–35 minutes

orange and almond torte

tarta de naranja y almendra

- **butter, for greasing**
- **flour, for dusting**
- **6 eggs, separated**
- **175 g (6 oz) caster sugar**
- **grated rind and juice of 1 orange**
- **175 g (6 oz) ground almonds**
- **75 g (3 oz) day-old breadcrumbs**
- **whipped cream, to serve**

SYRUP

- **juice of 3 oranges**
- **3 cardamom pods, bruised**
- **sugar**

1 Grease and base-line a 23 cm (9 inch) springform tin, then dust it lightly with flour. Beat the egg yolks, sugar and orange rind and juice until pale then stir in the almonds and breadcrumbs. The mixture at this stage is quite thick.

2 Whisk the egg whites until just stiff. Stir a spoonful into the cake mixture then carefully fold in the rest until evenly incorporated. Transfer to the prepared tin and bake in a preheated oven, 180°C (350°C), Gas Mark 4, for 30–35 minutes until risen and springy to the touch. Leave to cool in the tin for 5 minutes, then transfer to a wire rack to cool completely.

3 To make the syrup, warm the orange juice, cardamom pods and sugar in a small saucepan until the sugar has dissolved, then boil for 3 minutes until syrupy. Spike the cake all over with a skewer and pour over the syrup. Serve in wedges with whipped cream.

fried bread with honey and lemon

pan frito con miel y limón

- 300 ml (½ pint) milk
- 50 g (2 oz) clear honey
- 2 strips of lemon rind
- pinch of ground cinnamon
- 8 large slices of day-old bread, crusts removed
- 2 eggs
- vegetable oil, for shallow-frying

TO SERVE
- soured cream
- clear honey
- lemon wedges

1 Warm the milk, honey, lemon rind and cinnamon in a saucepan until almost boiling. Remove from the heat and leave to cool for 20 minutes.

2 Cut the bread slices in half diagonally to form triangles and dip each piece into the sweetened milk. Transfer the slices to a wire rack set over a tray and leave to dry for about 2 hours.

3 Beat the eggs and heat a shallow layer of oil in a frying pan. Dip the bread into the egg, then shallow fry for 1–2 minutes on each side until golden. Serve with soured cream, a drizzle of honey and a squeeze of lemon juice.

This is a version of the French *pain perdu*, which the Spanish serve as a breakfast dish. It is, however, very good at any time of day.

Serves 8 / **Preparation time** 15 minutes + cooling and drying / **Cooking time** 15 minutes

3)

a bite more

galician pasties

savoury meatballs

warm chickpea salad

sweet and sour courgettes

squid with peppers and lemon

baked stuffed scallops

griddled prawns

marinated sardines

barbecued sardines

marinated seafood

stuffed baby squid

Serves 4–6 / **Preparation time** 30 minutes / **Cooking time** 30 minutes

galician pasties
empanadas gallegas

- 250 g (8 oz) cod, smoked haddock, or other well-flavoured white fish
- milk, for poaching
- 4 tablespoons oil
- 1 Spanish onion, finely chopped
- 1 green pepper, cored, deseeded and chopped
- 250 g (8 oz) Serrano or other raw smoked ham, finely chopped
- 1 tablespoon flour
- 300 ml (½ pint) oil, for frying
- salt and cayenne pepper

PASTRY
- 500 g (1 lb) plain flour
- ¼ teaspoon salt
- 175 g (6 oz) butter
- 4 tablespoons dry sherry
- about 2 tablespoons water

1 First make the pastry. Sift the flour and salt into a bowl and rub in the butter. Make a well in the centre and add the sherry and water; knead thoroughly until smooth. Cover and chill while preparing the filling.

2 Gently poach the fish in a little milk until just tender; strain and reserve the milk. Skin the fish.

3 Heat the oil in a frying pan and gently fry the onion and pepper until soft. Add the fish and ham. Stir in the flour and cook for a few minutes, then blend in a little of the reserved milk to make a fairly thick mixture. Season to taste with salt and cayenne pepper.

4 Roll out the pastry on a floured surface and cut out circles, about 15 cm (6 inches) in diameter. Place a generous tablespoon of the filling on one side of each circle. Dampen the edges and fold over the other half to make pasties.

5 Heat the oil in a large frying pan until a slight haze forms above it. Fry the pasties, a few at a time, basting rather than turning them over, until the pastry is crisp and golden brown. Remove and drain on kitchen paper. Serve hot.

Empanadas are popular all over Spain, and come in various shapes and sizes, with a variety of fillings. Huge empanadas are sold by the slice in the bars and restaurants of Galicia. This recipe is for a smaller pie, rather like a turnover, that is fried rather than baked.

savoury meatballs
albondigas

- **250 g (8 oz) lean minced beef**
- **125 g (4 oz) chorizo sausage, minced**
- **½ teaspoon salt**
- **2 garlic cloves, crushed**
- **½ teaspoon grated nutmeg**
- **1 tablespoon finely chopped parsley**
- **½ teaspoon dried oregano**
- **½ Spanish onion, finely chopped**
- **1 egg, beaten**
- **1 tablespoon dry sherry or brandy**
- **1 tablespoon flour**
- **pepper**
- **oil, for shallow-frying**
- **Romesco Sauce (see page 76), to serve**

1 Mix together all the ingredients in a large bowl, except for the flour and oil, seasoning with pepper to taste. Form the mixture into balls, about the size of walnuts, and toss them in the flour to coat thoroughly.

2 Heat the oil in a frying pan and fry the meatballs, stirring occasionally, for about 10 minutes or until evenly browned and cooked through. Remove with a slotted spoon and drain on kitchen paper. Serve hot with a bowl of romesco sauce for dipping.

Tip As well as making an excellent tapa, these spicy meatballs can also be served in a rich sauce as a main course.

warm chickpea salad

ensalada de garbanzos

- **5 tablespoons extra virgin olive oil**
- **1 red onion, finely chopped**
- **2 garlic cloves, crushed**
- **5 cm (½ inch) piece of fresh root ginger, grated**
- **2 x 400 g (13 oz) cans chickpeas, drained**
- **pinch of dried chilli flakes**
- **juice and finely grated rind of 1½ lemons**
- **1 bunch of coriander, chopped**
- **salt and pepper**
- **mixed ground cumin and paprika, to garnish**

1 Heat 1 tablespoon of the oil in a frying pan. Add the onion, garlic and ginger and cook gently for 5–7 minutes, stirring occasionally, until soft and translucent.

2 Add the chickpeas, dried chilli flakes and lemon rind and stir for about 30 seconds, then add the lemon juice and let the mixture bubble until it is almost dry. Add the coriander and season to taste with salt and pepper.

3 Transfer the mixture to a serving dish, pour over the remaining olive oil and set aside to cool. Sprinkle with a little of the cumin and paprika mixture and serve warm or at room temperature.

Tip With their nutty flavour, chickpeas make an ideal main ingredient in a salad. Warming them in the dressing means the chickpeas absorb all the flavours and, because they have a firm texture, there is no danger of them disintegrating.

Serves 4 / **Preparation time** 10 minutes / **Cooking time** 10 minutes

sweet and sour courgettes
albacines agridulces

- **3 tablespoons olive oil**
- **500 g (1 lb) courgettes, diced**
- **1 garlic clove, crushed**
- **1 red chilli, deseeded and finely chopped**
- **2 tablespoons raisins**
- **2 tablespoons salted capers, rinsed**
- **1 tablespoon sherry or balsamic vinegar**
- **1 teaspoon sugar**
- **2 tablespoons hazelnuts or blanched almonds, toasted and chopped**
- **2 tablespoons water**
- **salt and pepper**
- **chopped parsley, to garnish**

1 Heat the oil in a frying pan and stir-fry the courgettes over a high heat for about 3–4 minutes until golden. Lower the heat, add the garlic, chilli and a good sprinkling of salt and fry gently for a further 2–3 minutes until the garlic is softened.

2 Add the raisins, capers, vinegar, sugar, nuts, water and pepper to the pan. Cover and simmer for 5 minutes.

3 Taste and adjust the seasoning. Garnish the courgettes with the chopped parsley and serve hot.

Serves 4 / **Preparation time** 10–15 minutes / **Cooking time** 7–8 minutes

squid with peppers and lemon
calamares con pimiento y limón

- **500 g (1 lb) squid, cleaned**
- **3 tablespoons olive oil**
- **1 red pepper, cored, deseeded and chopped**
- **2 garlic cloves, chopped**
- **1 dried red chilli, crumbled**
- **finely grated rind of 1 small lemon**
- **3 tablespoons lemon juice**
- **1 tablespoon chopped parsley**
- **salt and pepper**

TO SERVE
- **lemon wedges**
- **country bread**

1 With a sharp knife, chop the squid tentacles roughly and cut the bodies into 1 cm (½ inch) thick rings.

2 Heat the oil in a deep frying pan, add the red pepper, garlic, chilli and lemon rind and cook gently, stirring occasionally, for about 5 minutes. Increase the heat to moderately high, stir in the squid and sauté for about 1–1½ minutes until it becomes opaque and just tender. Transfer to a warmed serving dish, sprinkle with salt, pepper and lemon juice to taste and scatter with parsley. Serve immediately with lemon wedges and country bread.

Serves 4 / **Preparation time** 15 minutes / **Cooking time** 20–25 minutes

baked stuffed scallops

vieras de santiago de compostela

- **4 large live scallops**
- **2 tablespoons chopped parsley**
- **2 garlic cloves, chopped**
- **2 onions, finely chopped**
- **large pinch of ground cloves**
- **a little grated nutmeg**
- **2 tablespoons fresh breadcrumbs**
- **1 tablespoon olive oil**
- **salt and pepper**

1 Wash and scrub the scallops. Open the shells by prizing them apart with a sharp knife, or put them on a baking sheet in a cool oven, 150°C (300°F), Gas Mark 2, for about 5 minutes until they open. Leave the oven on. Discard the hinge muscles, fringe and black intestinal thread. Ease out the white part with the coral attached. Clean the rounded half-shells thoroughly.

2 Chop the white and coral scallop flesh quite finely and mix with the parsley, garlic, onions, cloves, nutmeg and salt and pepper to taste. Fill the cleaned shells with this mixture. Sprinkle with breadcrumbs and olive oil and place on a baking sheet.

3 Increase the oven temperature to 220°C (425°F), Gas Mark 7, and bake the scallops for 15–20 minutes, or until lightly browned. Serve immediately, on a warmed plate.

Pilgrims who visited the shrine of Saint James at Santiago de Compostela in Spain wore scallop shells in his honour.

griddled prawns
gambas a la plancha

- **1 kg (2 lb) large raw prawns**
- **4 garlic cloves, sliced**
- **1 red chilli, deseeded and chopped**
- **4 tablespoons extra virgin olive oil, plus extra to serve**
- **1½ tablespoons lime juice**
- **salt and pepper**
- **lemon wedges, to garnish**
- **crusty bread, to serve**

1 Remove the heads from the prawns but leave the shells intact. Place the bodies flat on a board and, with a sharp knife, carefully cut down along the whole length of the prawn's back, without cutting all the way through and leaving the tail intact. Open the prawns out flat.

2 Discard the black vein from each prawn, then wash the prawns and pat dry. Place the prawns in a large bowl, add the garlic, chilli, olive oil and lime juice with a little salt and pepper. Cover and marinate for at least 1 hour.

3 Heat a griddle for 3 minutes until really hot. Add the prawns shell side down and fry for 3–4 minutes, in batches, until the flesh is cooked through. Turn them over and cook the second side for a few seconds. Transfer the cooked prawns to a large, warmed platter, drizzle over plenty of oil and serve with lemon wedges for squeezing and some crusty bread to mop up the juices.

In Spain, prawns and squid are often cooked very simply on a flat griddle. This method is known as *a la plancha*. Serve with some Romesco Sauce (see page 76) in a separate bowl.

Serves 4 / **Preparation time** 30 minutes + marinating / **Cooking time** 15–20 minutes

marinated sardines

sardinas en escabèche

- 20 small sardines, cleaned
- 3 tablespoons plain flour
- about 300 ml (½ pint) olive oil
- 2 garlic cloves, crushed
- ½ teaspoon powdered saffron
- 1 teaspoon ground ginger
- 4 tablespoons lemon juice
- 1 lemon, thinly sliced
- 4 small bay leaves
- salt and pepper
- crusty bread, to serve

1 Dust the sardines evenly with flour.

2 Heat 150 ml (¼ pint) of the olive oil in a frying pan and shallow-fry the sardines for about 3 minutes on each side until lightly golden. Drain on kitchen paper.

3 Put the sardines into a shallow serving dish. Mix the remaining olive oil with the garlic, saffron, ginger, lemon juice and salt and pepper to taste. Pour over the fish and put the lemon slices and the bay leaves on top. Cover the sardines and leave to marinate in the refrigerator for 24 hours, turning them from time to time.

4 Remove the sardines from the marinade and serve with crusty bread.

Serves 4 / **Preparation time** 10 minutes + marinating / **Cooking time** 15–20 minutes

barbecued sardines

sardinas a la parilla

- **2 red peppers**
- **extra virgin olive oil**
- **white wine vinegar**
- **16 fresh sardines, scaled and gutted (see tip)**
- **sea salt and pepper**
- **tomato and onion salad, to serve**

1 First skin the peppers. Put the whole peppers under a preheated hot grill, cook and turn until charred all over, then transfer them to a plastic bag and leave to cool. Peel and discard the skin and seeds, and cut the flesh into thin strips, mixing them with some oil, vinegar and salt and pepper.

2 Meanwhile, wash and dry the sardines, place them on a large platter and sprinkle liberally with sea salt. Cover and set aside for 1 hour. Wash and dry again, brush with a little oil and barbecue or grill for 2–3 minutes on each side until cooked through. Serve the sardines hot with the peppers and a tomato and onion salad.

Tip To gut a sardine, make a slit all the way down the centre of the belly from the head to the tail. Scrape the guts out of the cavity, then wash well, inside and out.

marinated seafood
mariscos en escabèche

- **16 large fresh mussels, scrubbed**
- **250 g (8 oz) baby squid, cleaned**
- **250 g (8 oz) small raw prawns, peeled and deveined**
- **2 garlic cloves, chopped**
- **1 small red chilli, deseeded and chopped**
- **50 ml (2 fl oz) dry sherry**
- **1 tablespoon chopped basil, to garnish**
- **bread, to serve**

MARINADE

- **150 ml (¼ pint) extra virgin olive oil**
- **2 shallots, chopped**
- **3 tablespoons white wine vinegar**
- **pinch of sugar**
- **1 tablespoon capers in brine, drained and chopped**
- **salt and pepper**

Escabèche means 'marinated' and is a classic tapas dish. Other fish or many types of vegetables can be cooked this way as well as all types of seafood.

1 First prepare the seafood. Remove any beards still attached to the mussels. Cut the squid bodies into rings and cut the tentacles in half. Wash and dry the prawns.

2 Put the mussels into a saucepan with the garlic, chilli and sherry, cover and steam for 4–5 minutes until they are all open (discard any that remain closed). Remove the mussels with a slotted spoon and put them into a bowl.

3 Poach the prawns in the mussel liquid for 4–5 minutes until cooked. Remove with a slotted spoon and add to the mussels. Poach the squid for about 2–3 minutes until cooked then transfer to the bowl of seafood. Reserve 2 tablespoons of the cooking liquid and leave the seafood to cool.

4 Combine all the marinade ingredients and stir in the reserved poaching liquid. Pour over the cold seafood, toss well and chill for several hours.

5 Allow the escabèche to return to room temperature about 1 hour before serving. Scatter the basil over the escabèche and serve with bread.

Serves 4 / **Preparation time** 25–30 minutes + cooling and chilling / **Cooking time** 15 minutes

stuffed baby squid
calamares rellenos

- 12 baby squid, about 12 cm (5 inches) long, cleaned
- 5 tablespoons extra virgin olive oil
- 1 small onion, finely chopped
- 2 garlic cloves, crushed
- 1 teaspoon chopped sage
- grated rind and juice of ½ lemon
- 50 g (2 oz) fresh white breadcrumbs
- 25 g (1 oz) anchovies, chopped
- 2 tablespoons chopped parsley
- 25 g (1 oz) pine nuts, toasted and chopped
- 50 ml (2 fl oz) dry white wine
- pepper

1 Remove and reserve the squid tentacles, wash the body cavities and pat dry with kitchen paper.

2 Heat 1 tablespoon of the oil in a frying pan and fry the onion, garlic, sage and lemon rind for 5 minutes. Transfer to a bowl and stir in the breadcrumbs, anchovies, parsley, pine nuts, lemon juice, chopped squid tentacles and plenty of pepper.

3 Use the mixture to stuff the squid bodies about two-thirds full and secure the tops with wooden cocktail sticks. Transfer the stuffed squid to a baking dish, drizzle over the wine and the remaining oil and bake in a preheated oven, 230°C (450°F), Gas Mark 8, for 20 minutes. Serve immediately.

Tip Do not over-stuff the squid as the filling expands during cooking and the squid may split.

Serves 4–6 / **Preparation time** 20 minutes / **Cooking time** 25 minutes

4) little meals

seafood soup

clam, potato and bean soup

cold vegetable soup

baked eggs with pepper
  and chorizo

grilled mediterranean vegetables

green bean and potato salad

stuffed peppers

hake with peppers

black rice with squid

spanish pasta with mussels

paella

kidneys cooked with sherry

catalan pork stew

chicken in garlic sauce

basque-style chicken with ham

Serves 4–6 / **Preparation time** 30 minutes / **Cooking time** 50 minutes

seafood soup
sopa de mariscos

- a few saffron threads
- 150 ml (¼ pint) boiling fish stock
- 4 tablespoons olive oil
- 1 onion, chopped
- 2 garlic cloves, crushed
- 1 tablespoon chopped thyme
- ¼ teaspoon dried chilli flakes
- 100 ml (3½ fl oz) dry sherry
- 400 g (13 oz) can chopped tomatoes
- 2 small cooked lobsters, about 475 g (15 oz) each
- 500 g (1 lb) monkfish fillet
- 2 tablespoons plain flour
- 12 large raw prawns, peeled
- 500 g (1 lb) fresh mussels
- 500 g (1 lb) fresh clams
- 50 g (2 oz) ground toasted almonds
- 1 tablespoon sherry vinegar
- salt and pepper
- crusty bread, to serve

1 Soak the saffron threads in the boiling fish stock for 10 minutes. While they are soaking, heat half of the oil in a large flameproof casserole and fry the onion, garlic, thyme and chilli flakes for about 10 minutes, until lightly golden.

2 Pour in the sherry and boil rapidly until reduced by half, then add the tomatoes, the saffron-infused stock and a little salt and pepper. Bring to the boil and simmer, covered, for 20 minutes. Transfer 150 ml (¼ pint) of the broth to a bowl and set aside.

3 To prepare the seafood, discard the lobster heads, cut the bodies in half lengthways and separate the claws. Cut the monkfish into cubes and dust lightly with flour. Wash and devein the prawns. Scrub the mussels and clams. Add the seafood to the casserole and return to the boil, stirring well. Cover and simmer for a further 10 minutes, or until all the seafood is cooked.

4 Combine the ground almonds, vinegar, the remaining oil and reserved broth and stir them into the soup, then heat through for 5 minutes until thickened. Serve with crusty bread.

Tip Vary the seafood to suit your taste or what is available when you come to make the soup. Try using langoustines instead of the lobsters or use cod instead of monkfish, for example.

clam, potato and bean soup
sopa de almejas

- 2 tablespoons olive oil
- 125 g (4 oz) piece of unsmoked pancetta, diced
- 1 onion, chopped
- 375 g (12 oz) potatoes, cubed
- 1 leek, sliced
- 2 garlic cloves, crushed
- 1 tablespoon chopped rosemary
- 2 bay leaves
- 400 g (13 oz) can cannellini or white haricot beans, drained
- 900 ml (1½ pints) vegetable stock
- 1 kg (2 lb) small clams or mussels, scrubbed
- salt and pepper
- crusty bread, to serve

GARLIC AND PARSLEY OIL

- 150 ml (¼ pint) extra virgin olive oil
- 2 large garlic cloves, sliced
- ¼ teaspoon salt
- 1 tablespoon chopped parsley

1 Heat the oil in a large saucepan and fry the pancetta for 5 minutes, until golden. Remove from the pan with a slotted spoon. Add the onion, potatoes, leek, garlic, rosemary and bay leaves to the pan and sauté gently for 10 minutes, until softened. Add the beans and stock, bring to the boil and simmer gently for 20 minutes, until the vegetables are tender.

2 Meanwhile, prepare the garlic and parsley oil. Heat the oil with the garlic and salt in a small pan and simmer gently for 3 minutes. Leave to cool, then stir in the parsley. Set aside.

3 Transfer half of the soup to a blender and blend until really smooth, then pour it back into the pan and season with salt and pepper to taste. Stir in the clams or mussels and add the pancetta to the soup. Simmer gently for about 5 minutes until the shellfish are open (discard any that remain closed). Spoon the soup into bowls and serve drizzled with the garlic and parsley oil, accompanied by crusty bread.

Serves 6–8 / **Preparation time** 15–20 minutes + chilling

cold vegetable soup
gazpacho

- 1 garlic clove, halved
- 1 litre (1¾ pints) tomato juice
- 3 tablespoons olive oil
- 2 tablespoons lemon juice
- 2 teaspoons sugar
- 150 g (5 oz) cucumber, peeled and diced
- 75 g (3 oz) mild red onion or spring onions, chopped
- 150 g (5 oz) red pepper, cored, deseeded and diced
- 75 g (3 oz) avocado, stoned, peeled and diced
- 2 tablespoons chopped mixed herbs, such as parsley, chives, basil and marjoram
- salt and pepper
- ice cubes, to serve

1 Rub the cut surfaces of the garlic over the bottom and sides of a large mixing bowl then discard the garlic. Pour the tomato juice into the bowl and add the oil, lemon juice, sugar and salt and pepper to taste. Lightly beat together, then cover and chill for at least 1 hour.

2 Beat the soup base again, then add the cucumber, onion, red pepper, avocado and herbs and stir gently.

3 Put ice cubes into individual soup bowls and ladle the soup over the top.

Tip If you like, this famous cold soup may be served with the diced ingredients – cucumber, onions, peppers and avocado – presented in separate bowls. Each diner can choose which to add to the basic tomato and herb soup.

Serves 4 / **Preparation time** 20 minutes / **Cooking time** about 40 minutes

baked eggs with pepper and chorizo
huevos a la flamenca

- **4 tablespoons olive oil**
- **2 large potatoes, diced**
- **4 slices of Serrano or other smoked ham**
- **1 onion, chopped**
- **1 red pepper, cored, deseeded and cut into strips**
- **125 g (4 oz) asparagus tips**
- **125 g (4 oz) peas**
- **4 tomatoes, skinned and chopped**
- **2 tablespoons tomato purée**
- **125 ml (4 fl oz) water**
- **4 eggs**
- **8 thin slices of chorizo sausage**
- **2 tablespoons chopped parsley**
- **salt and cayenne pepper**

1 Heat the oil in a large frying pan and sauté the potatoes until lightly browned. Remove with a slotted spoon and set aside.

2 Cut 2 of the ham slices into small pieces and add to the pan with the onion and pepper. Fry gently until the onion is softened.

3 Add the asparagus, peas, tomatoes and tomato purée. Stir in the potatoes and water, and season to taste with salt and cayenne pepper. Cover and cook over a low heat for 10 minutes, stirring occasionally.

4 Transfer the mixture to an oiled ovenproof dish or 4 large ramekins. Make hollows in the mixture and break each egg into a hollow. Arrange the chorizo and remaining ham on top and sprinkle with parsley. Cook in a preheated oven, 180°C (350°F), Gas Mark 4, for 15 minutes or until the whites of the eggs are just set. Serve hot.

grilled mediterranean vegetables

verduras a la plancha

- **1 small aubergine**
- **1 large courgette**
- **1 red pepper, cored and deseeded**
- **1 red onion**
- **3 garlic cloves**
- **1 teaspoon cumin seeds**
- **1 tablespoon chopped thyme**
- **1 tablespoon balsamic vinegar**
- **150 ml (¼ pint) extra virgin olive oil**
- **1 tablespoon chopped basil**
- **salt and pepper**

1 First prepare the vegetables. Cut the aubergine into 8 slices, the courgette into 5 mm (¼ inch) thick diagonal slices, the pepper into thick strips and the onion into thick wedges. Place in a large bowl.

2 Using a pestle and mortar, grind the garlic, cumin seeds and thyme to a paste and stir in the balsamic vinegar and 125 ml (4 fl oz) of the oil. Season with salt and pepper. Pour over the vegetables and toss well to coat.

3 Grill the vegetables under a preheated grill a few at a time for 2–3 minutes on each side until charred and tender.

4 Transfer the vegetables to a warmed serving platter, drizzle over the remaining olive oil and scatter over the basil. Serve warm.

Serves 4 / **Preparation time** 15 minutes / **Cooking time** 15 minutes

green bean and potato salad
ensalada de habas verdes y verduras

- **500 g (1 lb) new potatoes**
- **500 g (1 lb) green beans, trimmed and cut into 5 cm (2 inch) lengths**
- **1 onion, thinly sliced**
- **4 slices of Serrano ham**
- **2 tablespoons chopped parsley, to garnish**

DRESSING

- **6 tablespoons extra virgin olive oil**
- **2-3 teaspoons sherry vinegar**
- **1 garlic clove, thinly sliced**
- **½ teaspoon ground cumin**
- **pinch of sugar**
- **salt and pepper**

1 Bring a large saucepan of lightly salted water to the boil, add the potatoes and cook for 8 minutes, then add the beans and continue to cook for a further 4–5 minutes until they are both tender. Drain and refresh under cold water and pat dry.

2 Combine the beans, potatoes and onions in a large bowl. Whisk all the dressing ingredients together and mix with the vegetables. Arrange the slices of ham over the top and garnish with the parsley. Serve immediately.

Tip Choose a variety of new potato or a waxy salad potato for this dish to ensure a good, firm texture. Older, floury potatoes may crumble or fall apart.

stuffed peppers
pimientos rellenos

- **4 large red or green peppers**
- **1 tablespoon olive oil**
- **1 onion, finely chopped**
- **50 g (2 oz) streaky bacon, finely chopped**
- **175 g (6 oz) lean minced beef**
- **4 tablespoons breadcrumbs**
- **1 egg, beaten**
- **1 tablespoon chopped parsley**
- **salt and pepper**

SAUCE
- **2 tablespoons olive oil**
- **250 g (8 oz) canned tomatoes**
- **1 tablespoon tomato purée**
- **1 garlic clove, crushed**
- **1 teaspoon brown sugar**
- **1 tablespoon wine vinegar**

1 Cut the tops off the peppers and reserve. Scoop out the seeds with a spoon. Heat the oil in a saucepan and sauté the onion for 5 minutes. Stir in the bacon and beef and cook, turning, for 5 more minutes. Stir in the breadcrumbs. Remove the pan from the heat, stir in the egg and parsley and season with salt and pepper to taste. Stuff the peppers with this mixture, stand them upright in a deep ovenproof dish and replace the tops.

2 To prepare the sauce, gently heat the oil in a small pan, add the tomatoes and tomato purée and mix well. Add all the remaining ingredients, season to taste and bring to the boil. Lower the heat, cover and cook gently, stirring occasionally, for 10 minutes.

3 Pour the sauce over the peppers, cover and cook in a preheated oven, 160°C (325°F), Gas Mark 3, for about 40 minutes. Serve hot.

Serves 4 / **Preparation time** 15 minutes / **Cooking time** 30–40 minutes

hake with peppers
merluza con pimientos

- **4 tablespoons olive oil**
- **4 small red peppers, cored, deseeded and thickly sliced**
- **3 garlic cloves, peeled but left whole**
- **2 thyme sprigs**
- **pinch of hot paprika**
- **75 ml (3 fl oz) dry sherry**
- **4 potatoes**
- **4 x 175 g (6 oz) hake steaks**
- **2 bay leaves**

TO SERVE

- **crusty bread**
- **Allioli (see page 77)**

1 Heat the oil in a flameproof casserole, add the peppers, garlic, thyme sprigs and paprika and fry over a gentle heat for 15–20 minutes, stirring frequently, until browned and softened. Add the sherry and boil rapidly until it has reduced by half.

2 Meanwhile, parboil the potatoes for 10–12 minutes until nearly cooked. Refresh under cold water and cut into small cubes.

3 Stir the potatoes into the peppers with some salt and pepper. Season the hake steaks and arrange them on top, pressing them down into the peppers slightly. Add the bay leaves, cover the casserole and simmer gently over a low heat for 15–20 minutes, depending on the thickness of the fish. Leave the fish to rest for a few minutes before serving with crusty bread and allioli.

Serves 4 / **Preparation time** 15 minutes / **Cooking time** 25–30 minutes

black rice with squid

arroz negro con calamares

- **50 g (2 oz) butter**
- **400 g (13 oz) small squid, cleaned and diced**
- **1 large onion, finely chopped**
- **4 garlic cloves, crushed**
- **2 ripe tomatoes, skinned, deseeded and chopped**
- **250 g (8 oz) Spanish short-grain rice or risotto rice**
- **150 ml (¼ pint) dry white wine**
- **2 sachets squid ink (see below)**
- **600 ml (1 pint) fish stock**
- **salt and pepper**

1   Melt half of the butter in a saucepan and stir-fry the squid for 3–4 minutes until golden. Stir in the remaining butter, add the onion, garlic and tomatoes and fry gently for 5 minutes.

2   Add the rice and stir for 1 minute until the grains are coated and glossy. Pour in the wine and boil until reduced by half.

3   Stir in the squid ink and all the stock and season lightly with salt and pepper. Bring to the boil and simmer gently, uncovered, for 15–20 minutes until the rice is tender. Do not stir. Remove the pan from the heat, cover and leave to rest for 5 minutes. Taste and adjust the seasoning and serve hot.

Tip This dish of rice and squid cooked in squid ink is very popular throughout Spain. Small sachets of squid ink are available from most good fishmongers; two will be sufficient for this recipe.

spanish pasta with mussels

pastas con mejillones

- **500 g (1 lb) monkfish tail**
- **4 tablespoons olive oil**
- **1 onion, finely chopped**
- **4 garlic cloves, finely chopped**
- **500 g (1 lb) ripe tomatoes, skinned, deseeded and chopped**
- **¼ teaspoon saffron threads**
- **1.8 litres (3 pints) fish stock**
- **375 g (12 oz) dried fideus or capellini**
- **1 kg (2 lb) small mussels, scrubbed**
- **salt and pepper**
- **Allioli (see page 77), to serve**

Tip This dish comes from Catalonia and uses thin, short lengths of pasta called *fideus*. Spanish pasta is always cooked until really soft. If you can't find *fideus*, use *capellini* instead and break it into 5 cm (2 inch) lengths.

1 Wash and dry the monkfish tail and, using a sharp knife, cut through the bone to produce large chunks.

2 Heat half of the oil in a saucepan and fry the onion, garlic and tomatoes for 10 minutes. Add the monkfish, saffron threads and fish stock, bring to the boil and simmer gently for 5 minutes. Remove the fish and set aside. Continue to simmer gently for a further 25 minutes.

3 Meanwhile, heat the remaining oil in a flameproof casserole. Break the pasta into short lengths, add them to the hot oil and fry gently for 5 minutes, stirring constantly, until the pasta is golden.

4 Gradually stir in the tomato broth and simmer gently, stirring, until the pasta is cooked. Add the mussels, stir well and then add the monkfish. Cook for a further 5–6 minutes until the mussels have opened and the monkfish is cooked. Season with salt and pepper to taste and serve with the allioli.

Serves 4 / **Preparation time** 15 minutes / **Cooking time** 35–40 minutes

paella
paella

- **2 tablespoons olive oil**
- **1 small chicken, cut into 8 portions**
- **125 g (4 oz) bacon, diced**
- **1 large Spanish onion, chopped**
- **2–3 garlic cloves**
- **500 g (1 lb) tomatoes, skinned and chopped**
- **1 red pepper, cored, deseeded and chopped**
- **250 g (8 oz) Spanish short-grain rice or risotto rice**
- **pinch of saffron threads or powder**
- **600 ml (1 pint) boiling water**
- **75 g (3 oz) chorizo sausage, thinly sliced**
- **12 mussels, scrubbed and debearded**
- **12 cooked prawns in shell**
- **salt and pepper**
- **chopped parsley, to garnish**

1   Heat the oil in a paella pan or a large heavy-based frying pan, and fry the chicken and bacon until golden and just tender. Remove from the pan, add the onion and garlic and cook for 5 minutes or until golden brown.

2   Add the tomatoes and cook for 2–3 minutes, then add the red pepper and rice. Stir over a gentle heat for 1–2 minutes, mixing the rice with the onion mixture. Mix the saffron with the boiling water and pour over the rice. Season with salt and pepper. Cook until the rice is almost tender. Stir occasionally, adding more boiling water if needed.

3   Meanwhile, put the mussels in a saucepan with boiling water to cover. Shake the pan until all the shells have opened; discard any that remain closed. Return the chicken and bacon to the pan. Add the chorizo, mussels and prawns. Heat for 5–7 minutes. Garnish with parsley and serve hot.

Serves 4 / **Preparation time** 15 minutes / **Cooking time** 10 minutes

kidneys cooked with sherry
riñones al jérez

- **8 veal or lamb kidneys, prepared**
- **4 tablespoons lemon juice**
- **2 tablespoons olive oil**
- **1 garlic clove, crushed**
- **125 g (4 oz) smoked ham or pancetta, chopped**
- **50 ml (2 fl oz) dry sherry**
- **2 tablespoons chopped parsley**
- **salt and pepper**

1 Place the kidney halves in a bowl, add the lemon juice and set aside for 10 minutes.

2 Heat the oil in a large frying pan and when hot add the kidneys, garlic and ham and stir over a high heat for about 3–4 minutes until browned.

3 Add the sherry and simmer for a further 3–4 minutes until the sherry is reduced and the kidneys cooked through. Sprinkle over the parsley, season to taste with salt and pepper and serve.

Tip To prepare kidneys, cut them in half widthways and open out the two halves, then cut out the white cores using a small, sharp knife.

catalan pork stew
cocido catalán

- **150 ml (¼ pint) olive oil**
- **750 g (1½ lb) lean pork, cut into 2.5 cm (1 inch) cubes**
- **1 large onion, sliced**
- **2 garlic cloves, crushed**
- **500 g (1 lb) tomatoes, skinned and chopped**
- **1 green pepper, cored, deseeded and chopped**
- **1½ teaspoons paprika**
- **150 ml (¼ pint) chicken stock**
- **1 aubergine, sliced**
- **2–3 tablespoons seasoned flour**
- **salt and pepper**
- **1 tablespoon chopped coriander leaves, to garnish**

1 Heat 2 tablespoons of the oil in a large saucepan or flameproof casserole, add the pork and sauté gently until golden brown on all sides, turning occasionally. Remove from the pan with a slotted spoon and reserve.

2 Add the onion and garlic and cook until soft and golden. Return the meat to the pan and stir in the tomatoes, green pepper, paprika and stock. Season to taste with salt and pepper.

3 Bring to the boil, cover with greaseproof paper and a lid and simmer gently for 1 hour or until the meat is tender.

4 Dip the aubergine slices in seasoned flour. Heat some of the remaining oil in a large frying pan. When it is hot, fry the aubergine slices, a few at a time, until they are golden brown on both sides. Add more oil as required. Remove with a slotted spoon and pat dry with kitchen paper.

5 Serve the stew with the fried aubergine, garnished with coriander.

Serves 4 / **Preparation time** 10 minutes / **Cooking time** 30–40 minutes

chicken in garlic sauce
pollo al ajillo

- **50 ml (2 fl oz) olive oil**
- **1.5 kg (3 lb) chicken, cut into serving pieces**
- **1 head of garlic, separated into cloves, peeled and minced**
- **125 ml (4 fl oz) water**
- **4 tablespoons lemon juice**
- **a few saffron strands, crushed in a little warm water**
- **salt and pepper**

1 Heat the oil in a large, heavy-based frying pan. Add the chicken pieces and cook over a moderate heat for 10–15 minutes, turning frequently, until golden. Place the chicken in a large, shallow casserole. Season to taste with salt and pepper.

2 Pour off all but about 3 tablespoons of oil from the frying pan. Sauté the garlic in the pan. Add the water, stir well and bring to the boil. Pour over the chicken and add the lemon juice and saffron.

3 Cook, covered, over a low heat for about 15 minutes or until the chicken is tender and cooked through. Serve immediately.

basque-style chicken with ham

pollo vasco

- **4 tablespoons olive oil**
- **175 g (6 oz) smoked ham or streaky bacon, diced**
- **4 large chicken quarters**
- **4 onions, sliced**
- **3 garlic cloves, crushed**
- **2 green peppers, cored, deseeded and diced**
- **¼ teaspoon dried marjoram**
- **400 g (13 oz) fresh tomatoes, skinned and chopped, or canned tomatoes**
- **150-300 ml (¼-½ pint) chicken stock**
- **salt and pepper**
- **2 tablespoons chopped parsley, to garnish**

1 Heat the olive oil in a deep frying pan. Add the diced ham or bacon and sauté gently, stirring occasionally, until lightly browned. Remove from the pan with a slotted spoon and reserve.

2 Add the chicken quarters to the pan and cook, turning occasionally, until they are golden brown. Remove with a slotted spoon and keep warm. Add the onions and garlic and cook gently until soft and golden. Add the peppers and marjoram, cover and cook gently for 10 minutes.

3 Add the tomatoes and stock (300 ml/½ pint if you are using fresh tomatoes, or 150 ml/¼ pint if using canned tomatoes in juice). Season to taste with salt and pepper. Return the chicken and ham to the pan, cover and cook gently for 40–45 minutes, or until the chicken is cooked and tender.

4 Remove the chicken and transfer to a serving dish. Boil the sauce gently to reduce if necessary, until it is thick enough to coat the back of a spoon. Taste and adjust the seasoning and pour the sauce over the chicken. Sprinkle with parsley and serve.

Tip To skin fresh tomatoes, cut a cross through the skin at one end, place them in a large bowl and cover with boiling water. Leave for 2 minutes, then drain and slip off the skins.

5)
salsas
and dips

romesco sauce
salsa romesco

- **1-2 small dried chilli peppers, deseeded and halved**
- **25 g (1 oz) blanched almonds**
- **3 garlic cloves, finely chopped**
- **2 small tomatoes, chopped**
- **150 ml (¼ pint) olive oil**
- **1-2 tablespoons wine vinegar**
- **sea salt and paprika**

1 Soak the chilli in boiling water for about 5 minutes, then drain and chop.

2 Dry-fry the almonds gently in a frying pan, turning occasionally, until lightly golden.

3 Put the almonds in a food processor or blender with the chopped chilli and garlic. Process until blended, then add the tomatoes and process again, adding the oil and vinegar by degrees. Season to taste with salt and paprika. Pour into a bowl and serve with meat or fish.

This famous peppery Catalan sauce takes its name from the small hot peppers grown in the region. It is served with many dishes, especially grilled fish or meat.

Makes about 175 ml (6 fl oz) / **Preparation time** 15 minutes / **Cooking time** 2–3 minutes

allioli
allioli

- **6 garlic cloves**
- **½ teaspoon salt**
- **2 egg yolks**
- **250 ml (8 fl oz) olive oil**
- **2 teaspoons lemon juice**

1 Put the garlic and salt into a bowl, or mortar, and crush thoroughly to a smooth paste. Transfer to a mixing bowl if using a mortar.

2 Blend in the egg yolks. Gradually add the oil, drop by drop at first, beating constantly, and adding a little of the lemon juice from time to time. When the sauce starts to thicken, the oil may be added in a thin stream. Pour into a serving dish and serve with salad, meat or fish dishes.

Tip This Catalan garlic mayonnaise is popular all along the eastern Spanish coast and is eaten with many dishes. The name comes from the Latin *allium* for garlic and *oleum* for oil. Make sure all of the ingredients are at room temperature before you begin to make the mayonnaise.

Serves 4 / **Preparation time** 10 minutes

Serves 6 / **Preparation time** 20 minutes + chilling / **Cooking time** 30 minutes

aubergine dip
salsa de berenjenas

- **1 kg (2 lb) aubergines**
- **about 4 tablespoons olive oil**
- **about 3 tablespoons lemon juice**
- **2 garlic cloves, very finely chopped**
- **40 g (1½ oz) onion, very finely chopped**
- **1½ tablespoons very finely chopped red pepper**
- **salt and pepper**
- **warm pitta bread, to serve**

TO GARNISH
- **olive oil**
- **chopped parsley**

1 Prick the aubergines all over with a fork, put on a baking sheet and bake in a preheated oven, 350°F (180°C) Gas Mark 4, for about 30 minutes, until the skin is charred and blistered and the flesh feels soft when the aubergines are pressed. When they are cool enough to handle, remove and discard the stems and skin and squeeze the flesh gently to expel surplus liquid.

2 Chop the aubergine flesh so that it still has some texture. Place in a bowl and pour in the oil. Mix in most of the lemon juice and stir in the garlic, onion, red pepper and salt and pepper. Taste and add more lemon juice, if necessary. Cover and chill in the refrigerator for several hours.

3 Return the dip to room temperature a short while before serving so that the purée is not too cold. Spoon it into a flat dish and make a few swirls in the surface with the back of a spoon. Pour a thin trickle of olive oil into the swirls and garnish with chopped parsley. Serve with warm pitta bread.

Serves 4 / **Preparation time** 10 minutes + infusing / **Cooking time** 6 minutes

smoky tomato sauce

salsa ahumada de tomate

- **4 ripe tomatoes**
- **1 small onion, finely chopped**
- **1 red chilli, deseeded and finely chopped**
- **1 garlic clove, crushed**
- **4 tablespoons chopped coriander**
- **2 tablespoons extra virgin olive oil**
- **1 tablespoon lime juice**
- **salt and pepper**

1 Using tongs, hold the tomatoes over a gas flame and char well on all sides. Alternatively, char quickly under a very hot grill. Cool slightly and then peel and discard the skins. Halve the tomatoes, remove the seeds and finely chop the flesh.

2 Put the flesh into a bowl and stir in all the remaining ingredients. Season to taste with salt and pepper, cover and leave to infuse for several hours. Serve as an accompaniment or as a dip.

(The charring of the tomato skins adds a wonderfully intense smoky flavour to this salsa.)